My First E-Mail Guide

Chris Oxlade

Heinemann Library

Chicago, Illinois

© 2007 Heinemann Library
a division of Reed Elsevier Inc.
Chicago, Illinois

Customer Service 888-454-2279
Visit our website at www.heinemannraintree.com

Designed by Philippa Jenkins
Illustrations by Tower Designs (UK) Ltd
Picture research by Melissa Allison
Production by Duncan Gilbert

Originated by Dot Gradations
Printed and bound in China by South China
Printing Co. Ltd

11 10 09 08 07
10 9 8 7 6 5 4 3 2 1

ISBN: 978-1-4329-0017-5 (hardcover)
       978-1-4329-0021-2 (paperback)

Library of Congress Cataloguing-in-Publication Data
Oxlade, Chris
   My First E-Mail Guide / Chris Oxlade.
      p. cm. -- (My First Computer Guides)
   Includes bibliographical references and index.
   ISBN 978-1-4329-0017-5 (hc)
   -- ISBN 978-1 4329-0021-2 (pb)
   1. Electronic mail systems--Juvenile literature.
I. Title.

TK5105.73.O95 2007
004.692--dc22
                2006100904

Acknowledgements
The publishers would like to thank the following for
permission to reproduce photographs: Alamy pp. **5**
right (BananaStock), **27** (Helene Rogers); Corbis
pp. **24** (RF), **20** (Renee Lynn); Getty Images pp. **5**
(Asia Images), **22** (Iconica), **9** bottom; Harcourt
Education Ltd pp. **7** inset, **9** top, **17**, **18**, **25** (Tudor
Photography); Masterfile pp. **14** (Chad Johnston), **29**
(Kevin Dodge), **23**; Superstock p. **28** (age fotostock)

Cover photograph of arrows on computer keys,
reproduced with permission of Corbis Royalty-Free.

The publishers would like to thank Robert Eiffert for
his assistance in the preparation of this book.

Contents

Some words are shown in bold, **like this**. You can find out what they mean by looking in the glossary.

What Is E-Mail?

An e-mail is a message, like a letter. You write it on a computer. You send it to another person's computer for that person to read. "E-mail" is short for electronic mail.

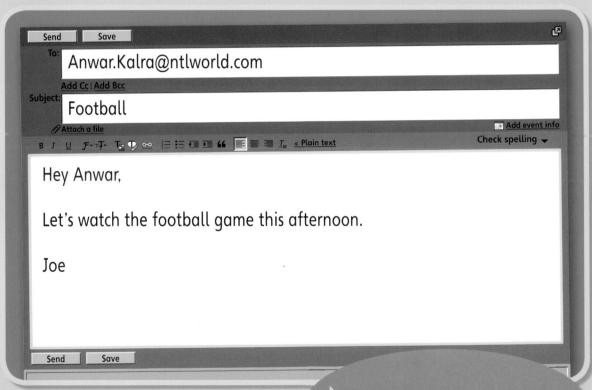

This is an e-mail message.

E-mail is an important way of sending messages today. Around the world, millions of e-mails are sent every minute.

Using E-Mail

People use e-mail to keep in touch with friends and family members. They also use it at work and school, to send information and to organize meetings.

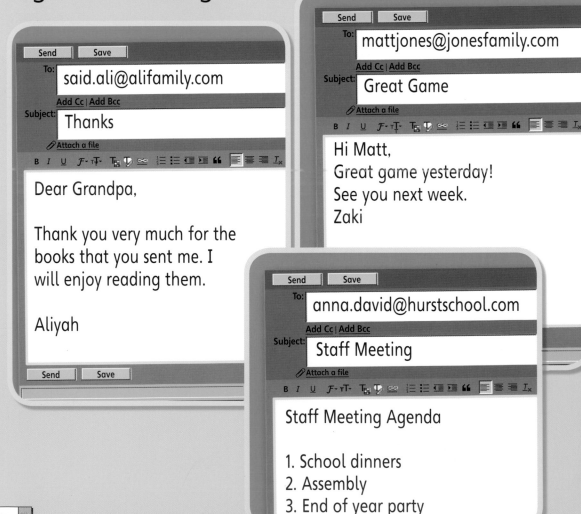

Send   Save
To: said.ali@alifamily.com
Add Cc | Add Bcc
Subject: Thanks
Attach a file

Dear Grandpa,

Thank you very much for the books that you sent me. I will enjoy reading them.

Aliyah

Send   Save

Send   Save
To: mattjones@jonesfamily.com
Add Cc | Add Bcc
Subject: Great Game
Attach a file

Hi Matt,
Great game yesterday!
See you next week.
Zaki

Send   Save
To: anna.david@hurstschool.com
Add Cc | Add Bcc
Subject: Staff Meeting
Attach a file

Staff Meeting Agenda

1. School dinners
2. Assembly
3. End of year party

E-mail can be better for sending messages than regular mail. An e-mail arrives in a few seconds, even when it is sent to the other side of the world. E-mail is also cheaper to send.

Send   Save

To: kathy.lee@leehome.com

Add Cc | Add Bcc

Subject: Fluffy

Attach a file

B *I* U F-ₜT- Tᵦ T̄ ⊝ ≔ ≣ ⊴ ⊵ 66 ☰ ☰ ☰ Tₓ « Plain text

Hello Aunt Kathy,
Here is a photo I took of my new pet rabbit, named Fluffy.
Love, Maya

Send   Save

You can easily send photographs with your e-mails.

The Right Address

An e-mail must be addressed to the right person, just like a letter. The address is called an **e-mail address**.

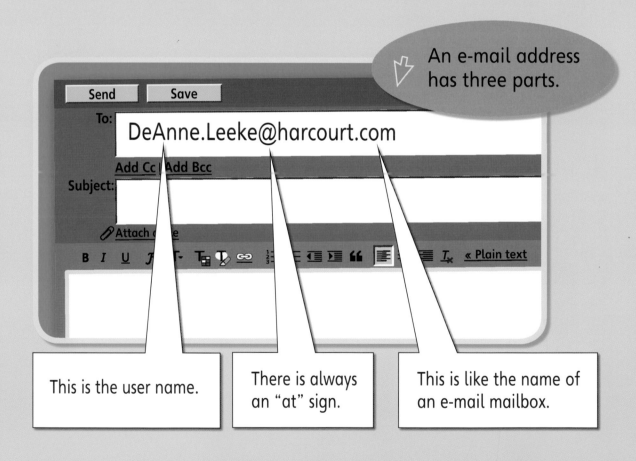

An e-mail address has three parts.

This is the user name.

There is always an "at" sign.

This is like the name of an e-mail mailbox.

People have to set up an e-mail address to send and receive e-mail. E-mail addresses are much shorter than postal addresses.

Joe Smith
10 Hill Street
Greenville , TX
80600

Mail is sometimes called "snail mail" because it is so slow compared to e-mail!

E-Mail Programs

You need an e-mail **program** on your computer
to send and receive e-mails. A program is
something that tells a computer what to do.

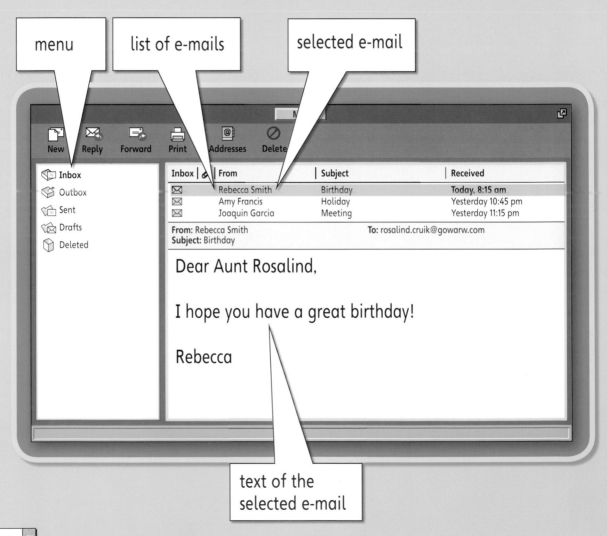

menu

list of e-mails

selected e-mail

text of the
selected e-mail

An e-mail program stores your e-mails. You can check to see all the messages you have sent or that people have sent to you.

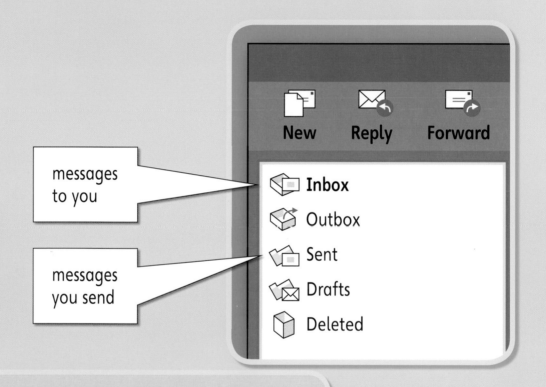

messages to you

messages you send

New   Reply   Forward

Inbox
Outbox
Sent
Drafts
Deleted

Activity
Go to a computer and click on the buttons for the Inbox, Outbox, and Sent box. What e-mails are in them?

Writing a Messag

When you write a new e-mail, first click on the "New" button. Then type in the **e-mail address** of the person you are sending the message to. You might find this person's address in the address book on the screen.

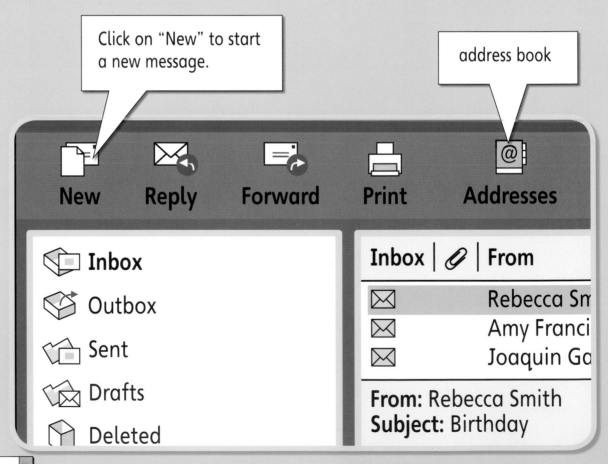

Click on "New" to start a new message.

address book

New   Reply   Forward   Print   Addresses

Inbox

Outbox

Sent

Drafts

Deleted

Inbox | 📎 | From

Rebecca Sm
Amy Franci
Joaquin Ga

From: Rebecca Smith
Subject: Birthday

Click in the "Subject" space and write what your message is about. Next, click in the message space. Now you can start writing your message.

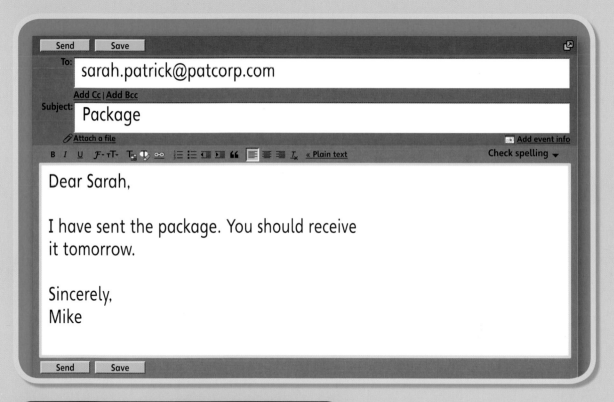

Send	Save		
To:	sarah.patrick@patcorp.com		

Add Cc | Add Bcc

Subject: Package

Attach a file   Add event info

B *I* U *F*-ₜT- Tₙ 🌐 ∞ ☰ ☰ ☰ ☰ " ☰ ☰ ☰ *Iₓ* « Plain text   Check spelling ▾

Dear Sarah,

I have sent the package. You should receive it tomorrow.

Sincerely,
Mike

Send	Save

STAY SAFE ☒

⚠ Never put your telephone number or other details in an e-mail to a person you do not know.

Being Polite

Remember, somebody will read the e-mails you write. Your e-mails should always be polite and easy to understand. Use complete sentences and the right punctuation.

Send | Save

To: peter.thomas@thomasfamilycom

Add Cc | Add Bcc

Subject: No News

Attach a file

IT WAS REALLY QUIET IN SCHOOL TODAY.

Never write e-mails in capital letters. It is like shouting in an e-mail.

You can use special e-mail pictures to say if you are happy, sad, angry, or surprised. These pictures are called **emoticons**. People who use e-mail will understand what emoticons mean.

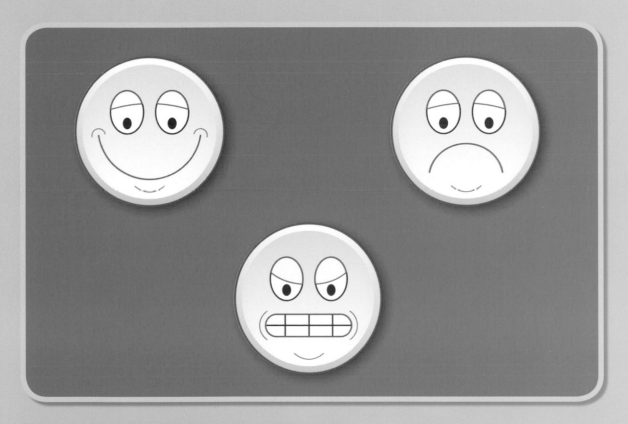

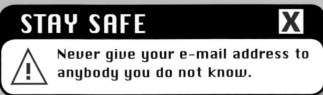

STAY SAFE ☒

⚠ Never give your e-mail address to anybody you do not know.

E-Mail Styles

When you write an e-mail, think about who you are writing it to. Imagine you are talking to this person as you write.

Simple notes are okay for friends.

Send   Save

To: alex.harwood@emailathome.com

Add Cc | Add Bcc

Subject: Weekend

Attach a file

B I U F·ₜT· Tₚ ∞ ⫶⫶ ⫶⫶ ⫷ ⫸ 66 ▤ ▤ ▤ Iₓ « Pla

Hi Alex,
How was your weekend?
We went to the zoo and saw a
camel. It looked so funny! Ha! Ha!
See you in class.
Kylie

Send   Save

Be careful in an e-mail to a teacher.

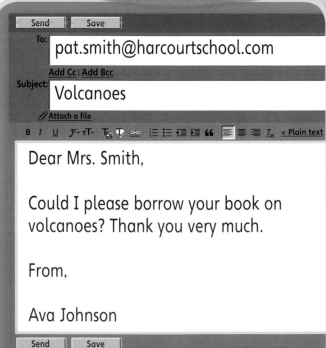

Send   Save

To: pat.smith@harcourtschool.com

Add Cc | Add Bcc

Subject: Volcanoes

Attach a file

B I U F·ₜT· Tₚ ∞ ⫶⫶ ⫶⫶ ⫷ ⫸ 66 ▤ ▤ ▤ Iₓ « Plain text

Dear Mrs. Smith,

Could I please borrow your book on volcanoes? Thank you very much.

From,

Ava Johnson

Send   Save

Sometimes it might be better not to use e-mail. Sometimes it is better to write a letter or card and send it in the mail. Sometimes it is better to talk on the phone.

Activity
How would you write an e-mail to a relative to say thank you for a present?

Send!

When you have finished writing your e-mail, you have to send it. Read your message first to make sure you have not made any mistakes. Check to make sure that the **e-mail address** is right.

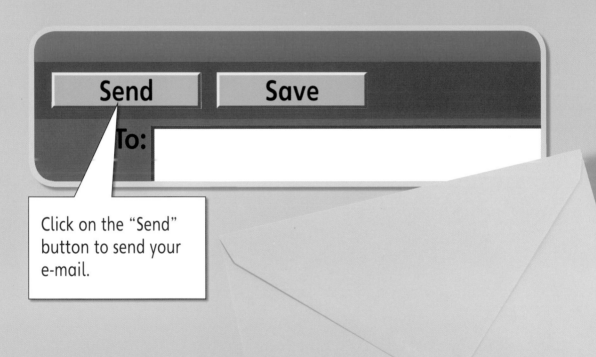

Send	Save

To:

Click on the "Send" button to send your e-mail.

After you press the "Send" button, the computer will tell you that your message has been sent. You might hear a noise when it has gone. The computer then moves the message into the Sent box.

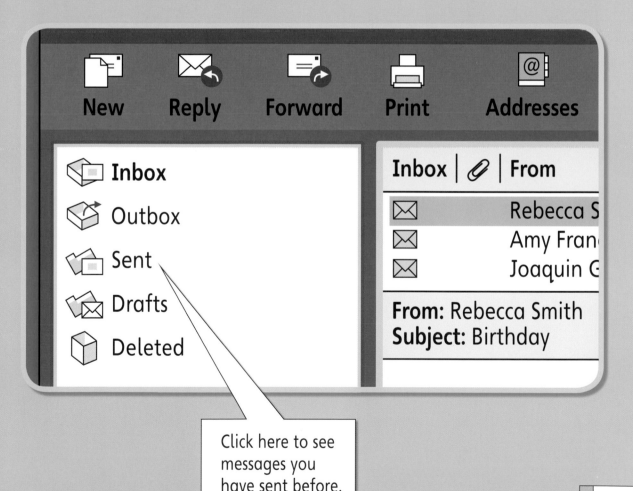

Click here to see messages you have sent before.

Getting Your Mail

To find out if anybody has sent you an e-mail, you ask the computer to look for you. Any new e-mail messages you get go into your Inbox.

Click here to see if you have any new messages.

New   Reply   Forward

Inbox
Outbox
Sent
Drafts
Deleted

You read a message by clicking on it in the Inbox. The message usually appears on the screen underneath.

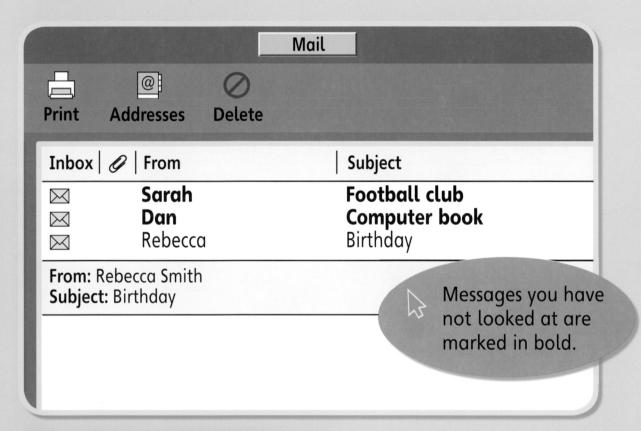

Mail		
Print	Addresses	Delete

Inbox ⬚	From	Subject
✉	**Sarah**	**Football club**
✉	**Dan**	**Computer book**
✉	Rebecca	Birthday

From: Rebecca Smith
Subject: Birthday

Messages you have not looked at are marked in bold.

STAY SAFE ❌

⚠ If anybody sends you an e-mail that upsets you, tell an adult right away.

Junk Mail

When you have an **e-mail address**, you often get e-mails from people you do not know. These are called **junk mail**, or **spam**. Most junk mail is trying to sell things.

Inbox 📎	From	Subject
✉	**Minnie Mouse**	**Geewhiz**
✉	**Big Fish**	**Unmissable**
✉	Rebecca Smith	Birthday

Junk mail may look interesting, but it is just trash.

Be very careful with junk mail. Click on the "Delete" button right away without reading it. It sometimes can harm your computer.

Ask an adult to help you get rid of junk mail.

Adding Attachments

You can send other files with your message, such as photographs, paintings, or word processor files. The files are called **attachments**.

Click on the paper clip to add an attachment.

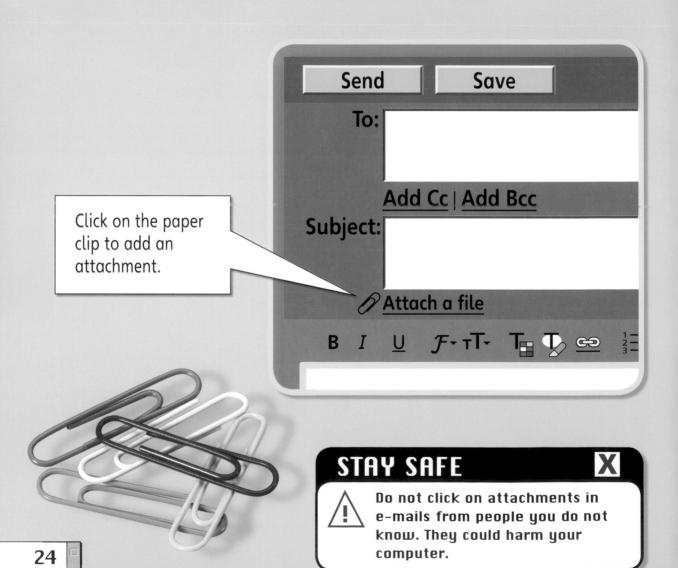

This e-mail has one attachment.

Activity

Ask someone to photograph you with a **digital camera**. Can you attach the photograph to an e-mail and send it to a relative?

Other Types of Messages

E-mail is not the only way of getting in touch by computer. Another way is called instant messaging. This is like talking to friends, but instead of saying things, you write them down.

 What you type shows up in the window. So do your friend's replies.

Instant Message

David: Are you going to the party this afternoon?

Chris: Yes, do you want a ride?

David: Yes, please, what time will you be here to pick me up?

Chris: About 6:30. What are you taking as a present?

David: A soccer ball. What are you taking?

Chris: A fun game.

Text messaging is similar to e-mail. Text messaging is when you send text messages from one mobile phone to another. You use phone numbers instead of **e-mail addresses**.

Staying Safe

E-mail is a great way to keep in touch with your family and friends. But it is important to stay safe when you use e-mail.

Remember:
- always delete **junk mail**
- never give your **e-mail address** to strangers, for example on a **Web site**
- never agree to meet up with a stranger who e-mails you.

Nothing beats talking to your friends in person.

Fun Facts About E-Mail

- The first e-mail was sent in 1971. It was very different from the e-mail we use today.
- Around 171 billion e-mails are sent every day.
- More than 1 billion people around the world use e-mail.

Find Out More

Nelson, Robin. *Communication Then and Now*. Minneapolis, MN: Lerner, 2003.

Ward-Johnson, Chris. *E-mail: A Magic Mouse Guide*. Berkeley Heights, NJ: Enslow, 2003.

Glossary

attachment file that you send with an e-mail message

digital camera camera that takes photographs that can be put onto a computer

e-mail address address that a person needs to send and receive e-mails

emoticons pictures you can add to e-mails to show how you feel

junk mail e-mail messages sent from people you do not know

program set of instructions that tells a computer what to do

spam junk mail from people you do not know

Web site collection of linked pages on the Internet about a subject or organization

Index